SIX CHARACTERS IN SEARCH OF AN AUTHOR

LUIGI PIRANDELLO

translated by
EDWARD STORER

LIST OF CHARACTERS

CHARACTERS OF THE COMEDY IN THE MAKING

The Father

The Mother

The Step-Daughter

The Son

The Boy

The Child
(The last two do not speak.)

Madame Pace

ACTORS OF THE COMPANY

The Manager

Leading Lady

Leading Man

Second Lady Lead

L'Ingénue

Juvenile Lead

Other Actors And Actresses

Property Man

Prompter

Machinist

Manager's Secretary

Door-Keeper

Scene-Shifters.

Act I

Daytime. The stage of a theatre.

NB. The Comedy is without acts or scenes. The performance is interrupted once, without the curtain being lowered, when the manager and the chief characters withdraw to arrange the scenario. A second interruption of the action takes place when, by mistake, the stage hands let the curtain down.

The spectators will find the curtain raised and the stage as it usually is during the day time. It will be half dark, and empty, so that from the beginning the public may have the impression of an impromptu performance.

Prompter's box and a small table and chair for the manager.

Two other small tables and several chairs scattered about as during rehearsals.

(*The* ACTORS *and* ACTRESSES *of the company enter from the back of the stage: first one, then another, then two together: nine or ten in all. They are about to rehearse a Pirandello play:* Mixing It Up. *Some of the company move off towards their dressing rooms. The* PROMPTER *who has the "book" under his arm, is waiting for* THE MANAGER *in order to begin the rehearsal.*)

(*The* ACTORS *and* ACTRESSES, *some standing, some sitting, chat and smoke. One perhaps reads a paper; another cons his part.*)

(*Finally,* THE MANAGER *enters and goes to the table prepared for him: His* SECRETARY *brings him his mail, through which he glances. The* PROMPTER *takes his seat, turns on a light, and opens the "book."*)

THE MANAGER	(*Throwing a letter down on the table.*) I can't see. (*To* PROPERTY MAN.) Let's have a little light, please!
PROPERTY MAN	Yes sir, yes, at once. (*A light comes down on to the stage.*)
THE MANAGER	(*Clapping his hands.*) Come along! Come along! Second act of *Mixing It Up*. (*Sits down.*)

(*The* ACTORS *and* ACTRESSES *go from the front of the stage to the wings, all except the three who are to begin the rehearsal.*)

PROMPTER	(*Reading the "book."*) "Leo Gala's house. A curious room serving as dining-room and study."
THE MANAGER	(*To PROPERTY MAN.*) Fix up the old red room.
PROPERTY MAN	(*Noting it down.*) Red set. All right!
PROMPTER	(*Continuing to read from the "book."*) "Table already laid and writing desk with books and papers. Bookshelves. Exit rear to Leo's bedroom. Exit left to kitchen. Principal exit to right."
THE MANAGER	(*Energetically.*) Well, you understand: The principal exit over there; here, the kitchen. (*Turning to ACTOR who is to play the part of Socrates.*) You make your entrances and exits here. (*To PROPERTY MAN.*) The baize doors at the rear, and curtains.
PROPERTY MAN	(*Noting it down.*) Right oh!
PROMPTER	(*Reading as before.*) "When the curtain rises, Leo Gala, dressed in cook's cap and apron is busy beating an egg in a cup. Philip, also dressed as a cook, is beating another egg. Guido Venanzi is seated and listening."
LEADING	(*To THE MANAGER.*) Excuse me, but must I

MAN	absolutely wear a cook's cap?
THE MANAGER	(*Annoyed.*) I imagine so. It says so there anyway. (*Pointing to the "book."*)
LEADING MAN	But it's ridiculous!
THE MANAGER	(*Jumping up in a rage.*) Ridiculous? Ridiculous? Is it my fault if France won't send us any more good comedies, and we are reduced to putting on Pirandello's works, where nobody understands anything, and where the author plays the fool with us all? (*The ACTORS grin. THE MANAGER goes to LEADING MAN and shouts.*) Yes sir, you put on the cook's cap and beat eggs. Do you suppose that with all this egg-beating business you are on an ordinary stage? Get that out of your head. You represent the shell of the eggs you are beating! (*Laughter and comments among the ACTORS.*) Silence! and listen to my explanations, please! (*To LEADING MAN.*) "The empty form of reason without the fullness of instinct, which is blind."—You stand for reason, your wife is instinct. It's a mixing up of the parts, according to which you who act your own part become the puppet of yourself. Do you understand?
LEADING MAN	I'm hanged if I do.

THE MANAGER   Neither do I. But let's get on with it. It's sure to be a glorious failure anyway. (*Confidentially.*) But I say, please face three-quarters. Otherwise, what with the abstruseness of the dialogue, and the public that won't be able to hear you, the whole thing will go to hell. Come on! come on!

PROMPTER   Pardon sir, may I get into my box? There's a bit of a draught.

THE MANAGER   Yes, yes, of course!

(*At this point, the* DOOR-KEEPER *has entered from the stage door and advances towards the manager's table, taking off his braided cap. During this manoeuvre, the* SIX CHARACTERS *enter, and stop by the door at back of stage, so that when the* DOOR-KEEPER *is about to announce their coming to* THE MANAGER, *they are already on the stage. A tenuous light surrounds them, almost as if irradiated by them—the faint breath of their fantastic reality.*)

(*This light will disappear when they come forward towards the* ACTORS. *They preserve, however, something of the dream lightness in which they seem almost suspended; but this does not detract from the essential reality of their forms and expressions.*)

(*He who is known as* THE FATHER *is a man of about 50: hair, reddish in colour, thin at the temples; he is not bald, however; thick moustaches, falling over his still fresh mouth, which often opens in an empty and uncertain smile. He is fattish, pale; with an especially wide forehead. He has blue, oval-shaped eyes, very clear and piercing. Wears light trousers and a dark jacket. He is alternatively mellifluous and violent in his manner.*)

(THE MOTHER *seems crushed and terrified as if by an intolerable weight of shame and abasement. She is dressed in modest black and wears a thick widow's veil of crêpe. When she lifts this, she reveals a wax-like face. She always keeps her eyes downcast.*)

(THE STEP-DAUGHTER, *is dashing, almost impudent, beautiful. She wears mourning too, but with great elegance. She shows contempt for the timid half-frightened manner of the wretched* BOY *(14 years old, and also dressed in black); on the other hand, she displays a lively tenderness for her little sister,* THE CHILD *(about four), who is dressed in white, with a black silk sash at the waist.*)

(THE SON *(22) tall, severe in his attitude of contempt for* THE FATHER, *supercilious and indifferent to* THE MOTHER. *He looks as if he had come on the stage against his will.*)

DOOR-KEEPER: (*Cap in hand.*) Excuse me, sir...

THE MANAGER: (*Rudely.*) Eh? What is it?

DOOR-KEEPER: (*Timidly.*) These people are asking for you, sir.

THE MANAGER: (*Furious.*) I am rehearsing, and you know perfectly well no one's allowed to come in during rehearsals! (*Turning to the* CHARACTERS.) Who are you, please? What do you want?

THE FATHER: (*Coming forward a little, followed by the others who seem embarrassed.*) As a matter of fact... we have come here in search of an author...

THE MANAGER: (*Half angry, half amazed.*) An author? What author?

THE FATHER: Any author, sir.

THE MANAGER: But there's no author here. We are not rehearsing a new piece.

THE STEP-DAUGHTER: (*Vivaciously.*) So much the better, so much the better! We can be your new piece.

AN ACTOR (*Coming forward from the others.*) Oh, do you hear that?

THE FATHER (*To THE STEP-DAUGHTER.*) Yes, but if the author isn't here... (*To THE MANAGER.*)... unless you would be willing...

THE MANAGER You are trying to be funny.

THE FATHER No, for Heaven's sake, what are you saying? We bring you a drama, sir.

THE STEP-DAUGHTER We may be your fortune.

THE MANAGER Will you oblige me by going away? We haven't time to waste with mad people.

THE FATHER (*Mellifluously.*) Oh sir, you know well that life is full of infinite absurdities, which, strangely enough, do not even need to appear plausible, since they are true.

THE MANAGER What the devil is he talking about?

THE FATHER I say that to reverse the ordinary process may well be considered a madness: that is, to create credible situations, in order that they may appear true. But permit me to observe that if this be madness, it is the sole raison d'être of your profession, gentlemen. (*The ACTORS look hurt and perplexed.*)

THE MANAGER (*Getting up and looking at him.*) So our profession seems to you one worthy of madmen then?

THE FATHER Well, to make seem true that which isn't true... without any need... for a joke as it were.... Isn't that your mission, gentlemen: to give life to fantastic characters on the stage?

THE MANAGER (*Interpreting the rising anger of the company.*) But I would beg you to believe, my dear sir, that the profession of the comedian is a noble one. If today, as things go, the playwrights give us stupid comedies to play and puppets to represent instead of men, remember we are proud to have given life to immortal works here on these very boards! (*The ACTORS, satisfied, applaud their MANAGER.*)

THE FATHER (*Interrupting furiously.*) Exactly, perfectly, to living beings more alive than those who breathe and wear clothes: beings less real perhaps, but truer! I agree with you entirely. (*The ACTORS look at one another in amazement.*)

THE MANAGER But what do you mean? Before, you said...

THE No, excuse me, I meant it for you, sir, who

FATHER were crying out that you had no time to lose with madmen, while no one better than yourself knows that nature uses the instrument of human fantasy in order to pursue her high creative purpose.

THE MANAGER Very well—but where does all this take us?

THE FATHER Nowhere! It is merely to show you that one is born to life in many forms, in many shapes, as tree, or as stone, as water, as butterfly, or as woman. So one may also be born a character in a play.

THE MANAGER (*With feigned comic dismay.*) So you and these other friends of yours have been born characters?

THE FATHER Exactly, and alive as you see! (THE MANAGER *and* ACTORS *burst out laughing.*)

THE FATHER (*Hurt.*) I am sorry you laugh, because we carry in us a drama, as you can guess from this woman here veiled in black.

THE MANAGER (*Losing patience at last and almost indignant.*) Oh, chuck it! Get away please! Clear out of here! (*To* PROPERTY MAN.) For Heaven's sake, turn them out!

THE FATHER (*Resisting.*) No, no, look here, we...

THE MANAGER (*Roaring.*) We come here to work, you know.

LEADING ACTOR One cannot let oneself be made such a fool of.

THE FATHER (*Determined, coming forward.*) I marvel at your incredulity, gentlemen. Are you not accustomed to see the characters created by an author spring to life in yourselves and face each other? Just because there is no "book" (*Pointing to the prompter's box.*) which contains us, you refuse to believe...

THE STEP-DAUGHTER (*Advances towards* THE MANAGER, *smiling and coquettish.*) Believe me, we are really six most interesting characters, sir; sidetracked however.

THE FATHER Yes, that is the word! (*To* THE MANAGER *all at once.*) In the sense, that is, that the author who created us alive no longer wished, or was no longer able, materially to put us into a work of art. And this was a real crime, sir; because he who has had the luck to be born a character can laugh even at death. He cannot die. The man, the writer, the instrument of the creation will die, but his creation does not die. And to live for ever, it does not need to have extraordinary gifts or to be able to work wonders. Who was Sancho Panza? Who was Don Abbondio? Yet they live eternally because—live germs as they were—they had the fortune to find a fecundating matrix, a fantasy which could raise and nourish them: make them live for ever!

THE MANAGER. That is quite all right. But what do you want here, all of you?

THE FATHER. We want to live.

THE MANAGER. (*Ironically.*) For Eternity?

THE FATHER. No, sir, only for a moment... in you.

AN ACTOR. Just listen to him!

LEADING LADY. They want to live, in us...!

JUVENILE LEAD. (*Pointing to* THE STEP-DAUGHTER.) I've no objection, as far as that one is concerned!

THE FATHER. Look here! look here! The comedy has to be made. (*To* THE MANAGER.) But if you and your actors are willing, we can soon concert it among ourselves.

THE MANAGER. (*Annoyed.*) But what do you want to concert? We don't go in for concerts here. Here we play dramas and comedies!

THE FATHER	Exactly! That is just why we have come to you.
THE MANAGER	And where is the "book"?
THE FATHER	It is in us! (*The ACTORS laugh.*) The drama is in us, and we are the drama. We are impatient to play it. Our inner passion drives us on to this.
THE STEP-DAUGHTER	(*Disdainful, alluring, treacherous, full of impudence.*) My passion, sir! Ah, if you only knew! My passion for him! (*Points to THE FATHER and makes a pretence of embracing him. Then she breaks out into a loud laugh.*)
THE FATHER	(*Angrily.*) Behave yourself! And please don't laugh in that fashion.
THE STEP-DAUGHTER	With your permission, gentlemen, I, who am a two months' orphan, will show you how I can dance and sing. (*Sings and then dances Prenez garde a Tchou-Thin-Tchou.*) Les chinois sont un peuple malin, De Shangaî à Pekin, Ils ont mis des écriteux partout: Prenez garde à Tchou-Thin-Tchou.
ACTORS AND ACTRESSES	Bravo! Well done! Tip-top!

THE
MANAGER   Silence! This isn't a café concert, you know! (*Turning to* THE FATHER *in consternation.*) Is she mad?

THE
FATHER   Mad? No, she's worse than mad.

THE STEP-
DAUGHTER   (*To* THE MANAGER.) Worse? Worse? Listen! Stage this drama for us at once! Then you will see that at a certain moment I... when this little darling here... (*Takes* THE CHILD *by the hand and leads her to* THE MANAGER.) Isn't she a dear? (*Takes her up and kisses her.*) Darling! Darling! (*Puts her down again and adds feelingly.*) Well, when God suddenly takes this dear little child away from that poor mother there; and this imbecile here. (*Seizing hold of* THE BOY *roughly and pushing him forward.*) does the stupidest things, like the fool he is, you will see me run away. Yes, gentleman, I shall be off. But the moment hasn't arrived yet. After what has taken place between him and me, (*Indicates* THE FATHER *with a horrible wink.*) I can't remain any longer in this society, to have to witness the anguish of this mother here for that fool.... (*Indicates* THE SON.) Look at him! Look at him! See how indifferent, how frigid he is, because he is the legitimate son. He despises me, despises him, (*Pointing to* THE BOY.) despises this baby here; because... we are bastards. (*Goes to* THE MOTHER *and embraces her.*) And he doesn't want to

recognize her as his mother—she who is the common mother of us all. He looks down upon her as if she were only the mother of us three bastards. Wretch! (*She says all this very rapidly, excitedly. At the word "bastards" she raises her voice, and almost spits out the final "Wretch!".*)

THE MOTHER (*To* THE MANAGER, *in anguish.*) In the name of these two little children, I beg you.... (*She grows faint and is about to fall.*) Oh God!

THE FATHER (*Coming forward to support her as do some of the* ACTORS.) Quick a chair, a chair for this poor widow!

THE ACTORS Is it true? Has she really fainted?

THE MANAGER Quick, a chair! Here!

(*One of the* ACTORS *brings a chair, the others proffer assistance.* THE MOTHER *tries to prevent* THE FATHER *from lifting the veil which covers her face.*)

THE FATHER Look at her! Look at her!

THE MOTHER No, no; stop it please!

THE (*Raising her veil.*) Let them see you!

FATHER

THE (*Rising and covering her face with her
MOTHER hands, in desperation.*) I beg you, sir, to
prevent this man from carrying out his plan
which is loathsome to me.

THE (*Dumbfounded.*) I don't understand at all.
MANAGER What is the situation? Is this lady your wife?
(*To* THE FATHER.)

THE Yes, gentlemen: my wife!
FATHER

THE But how can she be a widow if you are
MANAGER alive? (*The* ACTORS *find relief for their
astonishment in a loud laugh.*)

THE Don't laugh! Don't laugh like that, for
FATHER Heaven's sake. Her drama lies just here in
this: she has had a lover, a man who ought
to be here.

THE (*With a cry.*) No! No!
MOTHER

THE STEP- Fortunately for her, he is dead. Two months
DAUGHTER ago as I said. We are in mourning, as you
see.

THE He isn't here you see, not because he is
FATHER dead. He isn't here—look at her a moment
and you will understand—because her
drama isn't a drama of the love of two men

for whom she was incapable of feeling anything except possibly a little gratitude—gratitude not for me but for the other. She isn't a woman, she is a mother, and her drama—powerful sir, I assure you—lies, as a matter of fact, all in these four children she has had by two men.

THE MOTHER I had them? Have you got the courage to say that I wanted them? (*To the company.*) It was his doing. It was he who gave me that other man, who forced me to go away with him.

THE STEP-DAUGHTER It isn't true.

THE MOTHER (*Startled.*) Not true, isn't it?

THE STEP-DAUGHTER No, it isn't true, it just isn't true.

THE MOTHER And what can you know about it?

THE STEP-DAUGHTER It isn't true. Don't believe it. (*To THE MANAGER.*) Do you know why she says so? For that fellow there. (*Indicates THE SON.*) She tortures herself, destroys herself on account of the neglect of that son there; and she wants him to believe that if she abandoned him when he was only two years old, it was because he (*Indicates THE FATHER.*)

	made her do so.
THE MOTHER	(*Vigorously.*) He forced me to it, and I call God to witness it. (*To THE MANAGER.*) Ask him (*Indicates husband.*) if it isn't true. Let him speak. You (*To THE STEP-DAUGHTER.*) are not in a position to know anything about it.
THE STEP-DAUGHTER	I know you lived in peace and happiness with my father while he lived. Can you deny it?
THE MOTHER	No, I don't deny it…
THE STEP-DAUGHTER	He was always full of affection and kindness for you (*To THE BOY, angrily.*) It's true, isn't it? Tell them! Why don't you speak, you little fool?
THE MOTHER	Leave the poor boy alone. Why do you want to make me appear ungrateful, daughter? I don't want to offend your father. I have answered him that I didn't abandon my house and my son through any fault of mine, nor from any wilful passion.
THE FATHER	It is true. It was my doing.
LEADING MAN	(*To the company.*) What a spectacle!

LEADING LADY	We are the audience this time.
JUVENILE LEAD	For once, in a way.
THE MANAGER	(*Beginning to get really interested.*) Let's hear them out. Listen!
THE SON	Oh yes, you're going to hear a fine bit now. He will talk to you of the Demon of Experiment.
THE FATHER	You are a cynical imbecile. I've told you so already a hundred times. (*To* THE MANAGER.) He tries to make fun of me on account of this expression which I have found to excuse myself with.
THE SON	(*With disgust.*) Yes, phrases! phrases!
THE FATHER	Phrases! Isn't everyone consoled when faced with a trouble or fact he doesn't understand, by a word, some simple word, which tells us nothing and yet calms us?
THE STEP-DAUGHTER	Even in the case of remorse. In fact, especially then.
THE FATHER	Remorse? No, that isn't true. I've done more than use words to quieten the remorse in me.
THE STEP-	Yes, there was a bit of money too. Yes, yes,

DAUGHTER	a bit of money. There were the hundred lire he was about to offer me in payment, gentlemen.... (*Sensation of horror among the* ACTORS).
THE SON	(*To* THE STEP-DAUGHTER.) This is vile.
THE STEP-DAUGHTER	Vile? There they were in a pale blue envelope on a little mahogany table in the back of Madame Pace's shop. You know Madame Pace—one of those ladies who attract poor girls of good family into their ateliers, under the pretext of their selling *robes et manteaux.*
THE SON	And he thinks he has bought the right to tyrannize over us all with those hundred lire he was going to pay; but which, fortunately—note this, gentlemen—he had no chance of paying.
THE STEP-DAUGHTER	It was a near thing, though, you know! (*Laughs ironically.*)
THE MOTHER	(*Protesting.*) Shame, my daughter, shame!
THE STEP-DAUGHTER	Shame indeed! This is my revenge! I am dying to live that scene.... The room... I see it.... Here is the window with the mantles exposed, there the divan, the looking-glass, a screen, there in front of the window the little mahogany table with the blue envelope containing one hundred lire. I see it. I see it.

I could take hold of it.... But you, gentlemen, you ought to turn your backs now: I am almost nude, you know. But I don't blush: I leave that to him. (*Indicating* THE FATHER.)

THE MANAGER I don't understand this at all.

THE FATHER Naturally enough. I would ask you, sir, to exercise your authority a little here, and let me speak before you believe all she is trying to blame me with. Let me explain.

THE STEP-DAUGHTER Ah yes, explain it in your own way.

THE FATHER But don't you see that the whole trouble lies here. In words, words. Each one of us has within him a whole world of things, each man of us his own special world. And how can we ever come to an understanding if I put in the words I utter the sense and value of things as I see them; while you who listen to me must inevitably translate them according to the conception of things each one of you has within himself. We think we understand each other, but we never really do! Look here! This woman (*Indicating* THE MOTHER.) takes all my pity for her as a specially ferocious form of cruelty.

THE MOTHER   But you drove me away.

THE FATHER   Do you hear her? I drove her away! She believes I really sent her away.

THE MOTHER   You know how to talk, and I don't; but, believe me sir, (*To* THE MANAGER.) after he had married me... who knows why?... I was a poor insignificant woman....

THE FATHER   But, good Heavens! it was just for your humility that I married you. I loved this simplicity in you. (*He stops when he sees she makes signs to contradict him, opens his arms wide in sign of desperation, seeing how hopeless it is to make himself understood.*) You see she denies it. Her mental deafness, believe me, is phenomenal, the limit (*Touches his forehead.*) deaf, deaf, mentally deaf! She has plenty of feeling. Oh yes, a good heart for the children; but the brain—deaf, to the point of desperation—!

THE STEP-DAUGHTER   Yes, but ask him how his intelligence has helped us.

THE FATHER   If we could see all the evil that may spring from good, what should we do? (*At this point the* LEADING LADY *who is biting her lips with rage at seeing the* LEADING MAN *flirting with* THE STEP-DAUGHTER, *comes forward and says to* THE MANAGER.)

LEADING LADY	Excuse me, but are we going to rehearse today?
THE MANAGER	Of course, of course; but let's hear them out.
JUVENILE LEAD	This is something quite new.
L'INGÉNUE	Most interesting!
LEADING LADY	Yes, for the people who like that kind of thing. (*Casts a glance at* LEADING MAN.)
THE MANAGER	(*To* THE FATHER.) You must please explain yourself quite clearly. (*Sits down.*)
THE FATHER	Very well then: listen! I had in my service a poor man, a clerk, a secretary of mine, full of devotion, who became friends with her. (*Indicating t*THE MOTHER.) They understood one another, were kindred souls in fact, without, however, the least suspicion of any evil existing. They were incapable even of thinking of it.
THE STEP-DAUGHTER	So he thought of it—for them!
THE FATHER	That's not true. I meant to do good to them—and to myself, I confess, at the same time. Things had come to the point that I could not say a word to either of them

	without their making a mute appeal, one to the other, with their eyes. I could see them silently asking each other how I was to be kept in countenance, how I was to be kept quiet. And this, believe me, was just about enough of itself to keep me in a constant rage, to exasperate me beyond measure.
THE MANAGER	And why didn't you send him away then—this secretary of yours?
THE FATHER	Precisely what I did, sir. And then I had to watch this poor woman drifting forlornly about the house like an animal without a master, like an animal one has taken in out of pity.
THE MOTHER	Ah yes…!
THE FATHER	(*Suddenly turning to* THE MOTHER.) It's true about the son anyway, isn't it?
THE MOTHER	He took my son away from me first of all.
THE FATHER	But not from cruelty. I did it so that he should grow up healthy and strong by living in the country.
THE STEP-DAUGHTER	(*Pointing to him ironically.*) As one can see.

THE FATHER	(*Quickly.*) Is it my fault if he has grown up like this? I sent him to a wet nurse in the country, a peasant, as *she* did not seem to me strong enough, though she is of humble origin. That was, anyway, the reason I married her. Unpleasant all this maybe, but how can it be helped? My mistake possibly, but there we are! All my life I have had these confounded aspirations towards a certain moral sanity. (*At this point* THE STEP-DAUGHTER *bursts out into a noisy laugh.*) Oh, stop, it! Stop it! I can't stand it.
THE MANAGER	Yes, please stop it, for Heaven's sake.
THE STEP-DAUGHTER	But imagine moral sanity from him, if you please—the client of certain ateliers like that of Madame Pace!
THE FATHER	Fool! That is the proof that I am a man! This seeming contradiction, gentlemen, is the strongest proof that I stand here a live man before you. Why, it is just for this very incongruity in my nature that I have had to suffer what I have. I could not live by the side of that woman (*Indicating* THE MOTHER.) any longer; but not so much for the boredom she inspired me with as for the pity I felt for her.
THE MOTHER	And so he turned me out—.

THE
FATHER

—well provided for! Yes, I sent her to that man, gentlemen... to let her go free of me.

THE
MOTHER

And to free himself.

THE
FATHER

Yes, I admit it. It was also a liberation for me. But great evil has come of it. I meant well when I did it; and I did it more for her sake than mine. I swear it. (*Crosses his arms on his chest; then turns suddenly to* THE MOTHER.) Did I ever lose sight of you until that other man carried you off to another town, like the angry fool he was? And on account of my pure interest in you... my pure interest, I repeat, that had no base motive in it... I watched with the tenderest concern the new family that grew up around her. She can bear witness to this. (*Points to* THE STEP-DAUGHTER.)

THE STEP-
DAUGHTER

Oh yes, that's true enough. When I was a kiddie, so so high, you know, with plaits over my shoulders and knickers longer than my skirts, I used to see him waiting outside the school for me to come out. He came to see how I was growing up.

THE
FATHER

This is infamous, shameful!

THE STEP-
DAUGHTER

No, why?

THE FATHER	Infamous! infamous! (*Then excitedly to* THE MANAGER *explaining.*) After she (*Indicating* THE MOTHER.) went away, my house seemed suddenly empty. She was my incubus, but she filled my house. I was like a dazed fly alone in the empty rooms. This boy here (*Indicating* THE SON.) was educated away from home, and when he came back, he seemed to me to be no more mine. With no mother to stand between him and me, he grew up entirely for himself, on his own, apart, with no tie of intellect or affection binding him to me. And then—strange but true—I was driven, by curiosity at first and then by some tender sentiment, towards her family, which had come into being through my will. The thought of her began gradually to fill up the emptiness I felt all around me. I wanted to know if she were happy in living out the simple daily duties of life. I wanted to think of her as fortunate and happy because far away from the complicated torments of my spirit. And so, to have proof of this, I used to watch that child coming out of school.
THE STEP-DAUGHTER	Yes, yes. True. He used to follow me in the street and smiled at me, waved his hand, like this. I would look at him with interest, wondering who he might be. I told my mother, who guessed at once. (*THE MOTHER agrees with a nod.*) Then she didn't want to send me to school for some days; and when

	I finally went back, there he was again—looking so ridiculous—with a paper parcel in his hands. He came close to me, caressed me, and drew out a fine straw hat from the parcel, with a bouquet of flowers—all for me!
THE MANAGER	A bit discursive this, you know!
THE SON	(*Contemptuously.*) Literature! Literature!
THE FATHER	Literature indeed! This is life, this is passion!
THE MANAGER	It may be, but it won't act.
THE FATHER	I agree. This is only the part leading up. I don't suggest this should be staged. She, (*Pointing to* THE STEP-DAUGHTER.) as you see, is no longer the flapper with plaits down her back—.
THE STEP-DAUGHTER	—and the knickers showing below the skirt!
THE FATHER	The drama is coming now, sir; something new, complex, most interesting.
THE STEP-DAUGHTER	As soon as my father died…

THE FATHER	—there was absolute misery for them. They came back here, unknown to me. Through her stupidity! (*Pointing to* THE MOTHER.) It is true she can barely write her own name; but she could anyhow have got her daughter to write to me that they were in need....
THE MOTHER	And how was I to divine all this sentiment in him?
THE FATHER	That is exactly your mistake, never to have guessed any of my sentiments.
THE MOTHER	After so many years apart, and all that had happened....
THE FATHER	Was it my fault if that fellow carried you away? It happened quite suddenly; for after he had obtained some job or other, I could find no trace of them; and so, not unnaturally, my interest in them dwindled. But the drama culminated unforeseen and violent on their return, when I was impelled by my miserable flesh that still lives.... Ah! what misery, what wretchedness is that of the man who is alone and disdains debasing liaisons! Not old enough to do without women, and not young enough to go and look for one without shame. Misery? It's worse than misery; it's a horror; for no woman can any longer give him love; and when a man feels this.... One ought to do without, you say? Yes, yes, I know. Each of

us when he appears before his fellows is clothed in a certain dignity. But every man knows what unconfessable things pass within the secrecy of his own heart. One gives way to the temptation, only to rise from it again, afterwards, with a great eagerness to reestablish one's dignity, as if it were a tombstone to place on the grave of one's shame, and a monument to hide and sign the memory of our weaknesses. Everybody's in the same case. Some folks haven't the courage to say certain things, that's all!

THE STEP-DAUGHTER   All appear to have the courage to do them though.

THE FATHER   Yes, but in secret. Therefore, you want more courage to say these things. Let a man but speak these things out, and folks at once label him a cynic. But it isn't true. He is like all the others, better indeed, because he isn't afraid to reveal with the light of the intelligence the red shame of human bestiality on which most men close their eyes so as not to see it.

Woman—for example, look at her case! She turns tantalizing inviting glances on you. You seize her. No sooner does she feel herself in your grasp than she closes her eyes. It is the sign of her mission, the sign by which she says to man: "Blind yourself, for I am blind."

THE STEP-DAUGHTER   Sometimes she can close them no more: when she no longer feels the need of hiding her shame to herself, but dry-eyed and dispassionately, sees only that of the man who has blinded himself without love. Oh, all these intellectual complications make me sick, disgust me—all this philosophy that uncovers the beast in man, and then seeks to save him, excuse him.... I can't stand it, sir. When a man seeks to "simplify" life bestially, throwing aside every relic of humanity, every chaste aspiration, every pure feeling, all sense of ideality, duty, modesty, shame... then nothing is more revolting and nauseous than a certain kind of remorse—crocodiles' tears, that's what it is.

THE MANAGER   Let's come to the point. This is only discussion.

THE FATHER   Very good, sir! But a fact is like a sack which won't stand up when it is empty. In order that it may stand up, one has to put into it the reason and sentiment which have caused it to exist. I couldn't possibly know that after the death of that man, they had decided to return here, that they were in misery, and that she (*Pointing to* THE MOTHER.) had gone to work as a modiste, and at a shop of the type of that of Madame Pace.

THE STEP-DAUGHTER	A real high-class modiste, you must know, gentlemen. In appearance, she works for the leaders of the best society; but she arranges matters so that these elegant ladies serve her purpose... without prejudice to other ladies who are... well... only so so.
THE MOTHER	You will believe me, gentlemen, that it never entered my mind that the old hag offered me work because she had her eye on my daughter.
THE STEP-DAUGHTER	Poor mamma! Do you know, sir, what that woman did when I brought her back the work my mother had finished? She would point out to me that I had torn one of my frocks, and she would give it back to my mother to mend. It was I who paid for it, always I; while this poor creature here believed she was sacrificing herself for me and these two children here, sitting up at night sewing Madame Pace's robes.
THE MANAGER	And one day you met there....
THE STEP-DAUGHTER	Him, him. Yes sir, an old client. There's a scene for you to play! Superb!
THE FATHER	She, the Mother arrived just then....
THE STEP-	(*Treacherously.*) Almost in time!

DAUGHTER

THE
FATHER

(*Crying out.*) No, in time! in time!
Fortunately I recognized her... in time. And I took them back home with me to my house. You can imagine now her position and mine: she, as you see her; and I who cannot look her in the face.

THE STEP-
DAUGHTER

Absurd! How can I possibly be expected—after that—to be a modest young miss, a fit person to go with his confounded aspirations for "a solid moral sanity"?

THE
FATHER

For the drama lies all in this—in the conscience that I have, that each one of us has. We believe this conscience to be a single thing, but it is many-sided. There is one for this person, and another for that. Diverse consciences. So we have this illusion of being one person for all, of having a personality that is unique in all our acts. But it isn't true. We perceive this when, tragically perhaps, in something we do, we are as it were, suspended, caught up in the air on a kind of hook. Then we perceive that all of us was not in that act, and that it would be an atrocious injustice to judge us by that action alone, as if all our existence were summed up in that one deed. Now do you understand the perfidy of this girl? She surprised me in a place, where she ought not to have known me, just as I could not exist for her; and she now seeks to attach to me a reality such as I could never suppose I should have to assume for her in a shameful and fleeting moment of my life. I feel this above all else. And the drama, you will see, acquires a tremendous value from this point. Then there is the position of the others... his.... (*Indicating* THE SON.)

THE SON (*Shrugging his shoulders scornfully.*) Leave me alone! I don't come into this.

THE FATHER What? You don't come into this?

THE SON I've got nothing to do with it, and don't want to have; because you know well enough I wasn't made to be mixed up in all this with the rest of you.

THE STEP-DAUGHTER We are only vulgar folk! He is the fine gentleman. You may have noticed, Mr. Manager, that I fix him now and again with a look of scorn while he lowers his eyes—for he knows the evil he has done me.

THE SON (*Scarcely looking at her.*) I?

THE STEP-DAUGHTER You! you! I owe my life on the streets to you. Did you or did you not deny us, with your behaviour, I won't say the intimacy of home, but even that mere hospitality which makes guests feel at their ease? We were intruders who had come to disturb the kingdom of your legitimacy. I should like to have you witness, Mr. Manager, certain scenes between him and me. He says I have tyrannized over everyone. But it was just his behaviour which made me insist on the reason for which I had come into the house—this reason he calls "vile"—into his house, with my mother who is his mother too. And I came as mistress of the house.

THE SON It's easy for them to put me always in the wrong. But imagine, gentlemen, the position of a son, whose fate it is to see arrive one day at his home a young woman of impudent bearing, a young woman who inquires for his father, with whom who knows what business she has. This young man has then to witness her return bolder than ever, accompanied by that child there. He is obliged to watch her treat his father in an equivocal and confidential manner. She asks money of him in a way that lets one suppose he must give it her, *must*, do you understand, because he has every obligation to do so.

THE FATHER But I have, as a matter of fact, this obligation. I owe it to your mother.

THE SON How should I know? When had I ever seen or heard of her? One day there arrive with her (*Indicating* THE STEP-DAUGHTER.) that lad and this baby here. I am told: "This is *your* mother too, you know." I divine from her manner (*Indicating* THE STEP-DAUGHTER *again.*) why it is they have come home. I had rather not say what I feel and think about it. I shouldn't even care to confess to myself. No action can therefore be hoped for from me in this affair. Believe me, Mr. Manager, I am an "unrealized" character, dramatically speaking; and I find myself not at all at ease in their company. Leave me out of it, I beg you.

THE FATHER   What? It is just because you are so that....

THE SON   How do you know what I am like? When did you ever bother your head about me?

THE FATHER   I admit it. I admit it. But isn't that a situation in itself? This aloofness of yours which is so cruel to me and to your mother, who returns home and sees you almost for the first time grown up, who doesn't recognize you but knows you are her son.... (*Pointing out the* THE MOTHER *to the* THE MANAGER.) See, she's crying!

THE STEP-DAUGHTER   (*Angrily, stamping her foot.*) Like a fool!

THE FATHER   (*Indicating* THE STEP-DAUGHTER.) She can't stand him you know. (*Then referring again to* THE SON.) He says he doesn't come into the affair, whereas he is really the hinge of the whole action. Look at that lad who is always clinging to his mother, frightened and humiliated. It is on account of this fellow here. Possibly his situation is the most painful of all. He feels himself a stranger more than the others. The poor little chap feels mortified, humiliated at being brought into a home out of charity as it were. (*In confidence.*)—: He is the image of his father. Hardly talks at all. Humble and quiet.

THE MANAGER Oh, we'll cut him out. You've no notion what a nuisance boys are on the stage....

THE FATHER He disappears soon, you know. And the baby too. She is the first to vanish from the scene. The drama consists finally in this: when that mother re-enters my house, her family born outside of it, and shall we say superimposed on the original, ends with the death of the little girl, the tragedy of the boy and the flight of the elder daughter. It cannot go on, because it is foreign to its surroundings. So after much torment, we three remain: I, the mother, that son. Then, owing to the disappearance of that extraneous family, we too find ourselves strange to one another. We find we are living in an atmosphere of mortal desolation which is the revenge, as he (*Indicating* THE SON.) scornfully said of the Demon of Experiment, that unfortunately hides in me.

Thus, sir, you see when faith is lacking, it becomes impossible to create certain states of happiness, for we lack the necessary humility. Vaingloriously, we try to substitute ourselves for this faith, creating thus for the rest of the world a reality which we believe after their fashion, while, actually, it doesn't exist. For each one of us has his own reality to be respected before God, even when it is harmful to one's very self.

THE MANAGER There is something in what you say. I assure you all this interests me very much. I begin to think there's the stuff for a drama in all this, and not a bad drama either.

THE STEP-DAUGHTER (*Coming forward.*) When you've got a character like me.

THE FATHER (*Shutting her up, all excited to learn the decision of THE MANAGER.*) You be quiet!

THE MANAGER (*Reflecting, heedless of interruption.*) It's new... hem... yes....

THE FATHER Absolutely new!

THE MANAGER You've got a nerve though, I must say, to come here and fling it at me like this....

THE You will understand, sir, born as we are for

FATHER the stage....

THE MANAGER Are you amateur actors then?

THE FATHER No. I say born for the stage, because....

THE MANAGER Oh, nonsense. You're an old hand, you know.

THE FATHER No sir, no. We act that role for which we have been cast, that role which we are given in life. And in my own case, passion itself, as usually happens, becomes a trifle theatrical when it is exalted.

THE MANAGER Well, well, that will do. But you see, without an author.... I could give you the address of an author if you like....

THE FATHER No, no. Look here! You must be the author.

THE MANAGER I? What are you talking about?

THE FATHER Yes, you, you! Why not?

THE MANAGER Because I have never been an author: that's why.

THE Then why not turn author now? Everybody

FATHER   does it. You don't want any special qualities. Your task is made much easier by the fact that we are all here alive before you. …

THE MANAGER   It won't do.

THE FATHER   What? When you see us live our drama.…

THE MANAGER   Yes, that's all right. But you want someone to write it.

THE FATHER   No, no. Someone to take it down, possibly, while we play it, scene by scene! It will be enough to sketch it out at first, and then try it over.

THE MANAGER   Well… I am almost tempted. It's a bit of an idea. One might have a shot at it.

THE FATHER   Of course. You'll see what scenes will come out of it. I can give you one, at once.…

THE MANAGER   By Jove, it tempts me. I'd like to have a go at it. Let's try it out. Come with me to my office. (*Turning to the* ACTORS.) You are at liberty for a bit, but don't stop out of the theatre for long. In a quarter of an hour, twenty minutes, all back here again! (*To* THE FATHER.) We'll see what can be done. Who knows if we don't get something really extraordinary out of it?

THE FATHER	There's no doubt about it. They (*Indicating the* CHARACTERS.) had better come with us too, hadn't they?
THE MANAGER	Yes, yes. Come on! come on! (*Moves away and then turning to the* ACTORS.) Be punctual, please! (THE MANAGER *and the* SIX CHARACTERS *cross the stage and go off. The other* ACTORS *remain, looking at one another in astonishment.*)
LEADING MAN	Is he serious? What the devil does he want to do?
JUVENILE LEAD	This is rank madness.
THIRD ACTOR	Does he expect to knock up a drama in five minutes?
JUVENILE LEAD	Like the improvisers!
LEADING LADY	If he thinks I'm going to take part in a joke like this....
JUVENILE LEAD	I'm out of it anyway.
FOURTH ACTOR	I should like to know who they are. (*Alludes to* CHARACTERS.)
THIRD	What do you suppose? Madmen or rascals!

ACTOR	
JUVENILE LEAD	And he takes them seriously!
L'INGÉNUE	Vanity! He fancies himself as an author now.
LEADING MAN	It's absolutely unheard of. If the stage has come to this... well I'm....
FIFTH ACTOR	It's rather a joke.
THIRD ACTOR	Well, we'll see what's going to happen next.

(*Thus talking, the* ACTORS *leave the stage; some going out by the little door at the back; others retiring to their dressing-rooms.*)

(*The curtain remains up.*)

(*The action of the play is suspended for twenty minutes.*)

Act II

The stage call-bells ring to warn the company that the play is about to begin again.

(THE STEP-DAUGHTER *comes out of* THE MANAGER'S *office along with* THE CHILD *and* THE BOY. *As she comes out of the office, she cries:*)

THE STEP-DAUGHTER — Nonsense! nonsense! Do it yourselves! I'm not going to mix myself up in this mess. (*Turning to* THE CHILD *and coming quickly with her on to the stage.*) Come on, Rosetta, let's run!

(THE BOY *follows them slowly, remaining a little behind and seeming perplexed.*)

THE STEP-DAUGHTER — (*Stops, bends over* THE CHILD *and takes the latter's face between her hands.*) My little darling! You're frightened, aren't you? You don't know where we are, do you? (*Pretending to reply to a question of* THE CHILD.) What is the stage? It's a place, baby, you know, where people play at being serious, a place where they act comedies.

We've got to act a comedy now, dead serious, you know; and you're in it also, little one. (*Embraces her, pressing the little head to her breast, and rocking the child for a moment.*) Oh darling, darling, what a horrid comedy you've got to play! What a wretched part they've found for you! A garden... a fountain... look... just suppose, kiddie, it's here. Where, you say? Why, right here in the middle. It's all pretence you know. That's the trouble, my pet: it's all make-believe here. It's better to imagine it though, because if they fix it up for you, it'll only be painted cardboard, painted cardboard for the rockery, the water, the plants.... Ah, but I think a baby like this one would sooner have a make-believe fountain than a real one, so she could play with it. What a joke it'll be for the others! But for you, alas! not quite such a joke: you who are real, baby dear, and really play by a real fountain this big and green and beautiful, with ever so many bamboos around it that are reflected in the water, and a whole lot of little ducks swimming about.... No, Rosetta, no, your mother doesn't bother about you on account of that wretch of a son there. I'm in the devil of a temper, and as for that lad.... (*Seizes* THE BOY *by the arm to force him to take one of his hands out of his pockets.*) What have you got there? What are you hiding? (*Pulls his hand out of his pocket, looks into it and catches the glint of a* revolver.) Ah! where did you get this?

(THE BOY, *very pale in the face, looks at her, but does not answer.*)

Idiot! If I'd been in your place, instead of killing myself, I'd have shot one of those two, or both of them: father and son.

(THE FATHER *enters from the office, all excited from his work.* THE MANAGER *follows him.*)

THE FATHER Come on, come on dear! Come here for a minute! We've arranged everything. It's all fixed up.

THE MANAGER (*Also excited.*) If you please, young lady, there are one or two points to settle still. Will you come along?

THE STEP-DAUGHTER (*Following him towards the office.*) Ouff! what's the good, if you've arranged everything.

(THE FATHER, THE MANAGER *and* THE STEP-DAUGHTER *go back into the office again (off) for a moment. At the same time,* THE SON *followed by* THE MOTHER, *comes out.*)

THE SON (*Looking at the three entering office.*) Oh this is fine, fine! And to think I can't even get away!

(*THE MOTHER attempts to look at him, but lowers her eyes immediately when he turns away from her. She then sits down.* THE BOY *and* THE CHILD *approach her. She casts a glance again at* THE SON, *and speaks with humble tones, trying to draw him into conversation.*)

THE MOTHER   And isn't my punishment the worst of all? (*Then seeing from* THE SON*'s manner that he will not bother himself about her.*) My God! Why are you so cruel? Isn't it enough for one person to support all this torment? Must you then insist on others seeing it also?

THE SON   (*Half to himself, meaning* THE MOTHER *to hear, however.*) And they want to put it on the stage! If there was at least a reason for it! He thinks he has got at the meaning of it all. Just as if each one of us in every circumstance of life couldn't find his own explanation of it! (*Pauses.*) He complains he was discovered in a place where he ought not to have been seen, in a moment of his life which ought to have remained hidden and kept out of the reach of that convention which he has to maintain for other people. And what about my case? Haven't I had to reveal what no son ought ever to reveal: how father and mother live and are man and wife for themselves quite apart from that idea of father and mother which we give them? When this idea is revealed, our life is then linked at one point only to that man and that woman; and as such it should shame them, shouldn't it?

(THE MOTHER *hides her face in her hands. From the dressing-rooms and the little door at the back of the stage the* ACTORS *and* STAGE MANAGER *return, followed by the* PROPERTY MAN, *and the* PROMPTER. *At the same moment,* THE MANAGER *comes out of his office, accompanied by* THE FATHER *and* THE STEP-DAUGHTER.)

THE MANAGER	Come on, come on, ladies and gentlemen! Heh! you there, machinist!
MACHINIST	Yes sir?
THE MANAGER	Fix up the white parlor with the floral decorations. Two wings and a drop with a door will do. Hurry up!

(*The* MACHINIST *runs off at once to prepare the scene, and arranges it while* THE MANAGER *talks with the* STAGE MANAGER, *the* PROPERTY MAN, *and the* PROMPTER *on matters of detail.*)

THE MANAGER	(*To* PROPERTY MAN.) Just have a look, and see if there isn't a sofa or divan in the wardrobe. …
PROPERTY MAN	There's the green one.

THE STEP-DAUGHTER No no! Green won't do. It was yellow, ornamented with flowers—very large! and most comfortable!

PROPERTY MAN There isn't one like that.

THE MANAGER It doesn't matter. Use the one we've got.

THE STEP-DAUGHTER Doesn't matter? It's most important!

THE MANAGER We're only trying it now. Please don't interfere. (*To* PROPERTY MAN.) See if we've got a shop window—long and narrowish.

THE STEP-DAUGHTER And the little table! The little mahogany table for the pale blue envelope!

PROPERTY MAN (*To* THE MANAGER.) There's that little gilt one.

THE MANAGER That'll do fine.

THE FATHER A mirror.

THE STEP-DAUGHTER And the screen! We must have a screen. Otherwise how can I manage?

PROPERTY That's all right, Miss. We've got any

MAN	amount of them.
THE MANAGER	(*To THE STEP-DAUGHTER.*) We want some clothes pegs too, don't we?
THE STEP-DAUGHTER	Yes, several, several!
THE MANAGER	See how many we've got and bring them all.
PROPERTY MAN	All right!

(*The PROPERTY MAN hurries off to obey his orders. While he is putting the things in their places, THE MANAGER talks to the PROMPTER and then with the CHARACTERS and the ACTORS.*)

THE MANAGER	(*To PROMPTER.*) Take your seat. Look here: this is the outline of the scenes, act by act. (*Hands him some sheets of paper.*) And now I'm going to ask you to do something out of the ordinary.
PROMPTER	Take it down in shorthand?
THE MANAGER	(*Pleasantly surprised.*) Exactly! Can you do shorthand?
PROMPTER	Yes, a little.
THE	Good! (*Turning to a STAGE HAND.*) Go and get

MANAGER   some paper from my office, plenty, as much as you can find.

(*The* STAGE HAND *goes off, and soon returns with a handful of paper which he gives to the* PROMPTER)

THE MANAGER   (*To* PROMPTER.) You follow the scenes as we play them, and try and get the points down, at any rate the most important ones. (*Then addressing the* ACTORS.) Clear the stage, ladies and gentlemen! Come over here (*Pointing to the Left.*) and listen attentively.

LEADING LADY   But, excuse me, we....

THE MANAGER   (*Guessing her thought.*) Don't worry! You won't have to improvise.

LEADING MAN   What have we to do then?

THE MANAGER   Nothing. For the moment you just watch and listen. Everybody will get his part written out afterwards. At present we're going to try the thing as best we can. They're going to act now.

THE FATHER   (*As if fallen from the clouds into the confusion of the stage.*) We? What do you mean, if you please, by a rehearsal?

THE   A rehearsal for them. (*Points to the* ACTORS.)

MANAGER

THE
FATHER

But since we are the characters....

THE
MANAGER

All right: "characters" then, if you insist on calling yourselves such. But here, my dear sir, the characters don't act. Here the actors do the acting. The characters are there, in the "book" (*Pointing towards* PROMPTER'S *box.*)—when there is a "book"!

THE
FATHER

I won't contradict you; but excuse me, the actors aren't the characters. They want to be, they pretend to be, don't they? Now if these gentlemen here are fortunate enough to have us alive before them....

THE
MANAGER

Oh this is grand! You want to come before the public yourselves then?

THE
FATHER

As we are....

THE
MANAGER

I can assure you it would be a magnificent spectacle!

LEADING
MAN

What's the use of us here anyway then?

THE
MANAGER

You're not going to pretend that you can act? It makes me laugh! (*The* ACTORS *laugh.*) There, you see, they are laughing at the notion. But, by the way, I must cast the

	parts. That won't be difficult. They cast themselves. (*To the* SECOND LADY LEAD.) You play the Mother. (*To* THE FATHER.) We must find her a name.
THE FATHER	Amalia, sir.
THE MANAGER	But that is the real name of your wife. We don't want to call her by her real name.
THE FATHER	Why ever not, if it is her name? Still, perhaps, if that lady must.... (*Makes a slight motion of the hand to indicate the* SECOND LADY LEAD.) I see this woman here (*Means* THE MOTHER.) as Amalia. But do as you like. (*Gets more and more confused.*) I don't know what to say to you. Already, I begin to hear my own words ring false, as if they had another sound....
THE MANAGER	Don't you worry about it. It'll be our job to find the right tones. And as for her name, if you want her Amalia, Amalia it shall be; and if you don't like it, we'll find another! For the moment though, we'll call the characters in this way: (*To* JUVENILE LEAD.) You are the Son; (*To the* LEADING LADY.) You naturally are the Step-Daughter.
THE STEP-DAUGHTER	(*Excitedly.*) What? what? I, that woman there? (*Bursts out laughing.*)

THE MANAGER (*Angry.*) What is there to laugh at?

LEADING LADY (*Indignant.*) Nobody has ever dared to laugh at me. I insist on being treated with respect; otherwise I go away.

THE STEP-DAUGHTER No, no, excuse me... I am not laughing at you....

THE MANAGER (*To THE STEP-DAUGHTER.*) You ought to feel honoured to be played by....

LEADING LADY (*At once, contemptuously.*) "That woman there."...

THE STEP-DAUGHTER But I wasn't speaking of you, you know. I was speaking of myself—whom I can't see at all in you! That is all. I don't know... but... you... aren't in the least like me....

THE FATHER True. Here's the point. Look here, sir, our temperaments, our souls....

THE MANAGER Temperament, soul, be hanged! Do you suppose the spirit of the piece is in you? Nothing of the kind!

THE FATHER What, haven't we our own temperaments, our own souls?

THE MANAGER Not at all. Your soul or whatever you like to call it takes shape here. The actors give body and form to it, voice and gesture. And my actors—I may tell you—have given expression to much more lofty material than this little drama of yours, which may or may not hold up on the stage. But if it does, the merit of it, believe me, will be due to my actors.

THE FATHER. I don't dare contradict you, sir; but, believe me, it is a terrible suffering for us who are as we are, with these bodies of ours, these features to see....

THE MANAGER. (*Cutting him short and out of patience.*) Good heavens! The makeup will remedy all that, man, the makeup....

THE FATHER. Maybe. But the voice, the gestures....

THE MANAGER. Now, look here! On the stage, you as yourself, cannot exist. The actor here acts you, and that's an end to it!

THE FATHER. I understand. And now I think I see why our author who conceived us as we are, all alive, didn't want to put us on the stage after all. I haven't the least desire to offend your actors. Far from it! But when I think that I am to be acted by... I don't know by whom. ...

LEADING MAN. (*On his dignity.*) By me, if you've no objection!

THE FATHER	(*Humbly, mellifluously.*) Honoured, I assure you, sir. (*Bows.*) Still, I must say that try as this gentleman may, with all his good will and wonderful art, to absorb me into himself....
LEADING MAN	Oh chuck it! "Wonderful art!" Withdraw that, please!
THE FATHER	The performance he will give, even doing his best with makeup to look like me....
LEADING MAN	It will certainly be a bit difficult! (*The* ACTORS *laugh.*)
THE FATHER	Exactly! It will be difficult to act me as I really am. The effect will be rather—apart from the makeup—according as to how he supposes I am, as he senses me—if he does sense me—and not as I inside of myself feel myself to be. It seems to me then that account should be taken of this by everyone whose duty it may become to criticize us....
THE MANAGER	Heavens! The man's starting to think about the critics now! Let them say what they like. It's up to us to put on the play if we can. (*Looking around.*) Come on! come on! Is the stage set? (*To the* ACTORS *and* CHARACTERS.) Stand back—stand back! Let me see, and don't let's lose any more time! (*To* THE STEP-DAUGHTER.) Is it all right as it is now?

THE STEP-DAUGHTER	Well, to tell the truth, I don't recognize the scene.
THE MANAGER	My dear lady, you can't possibly suppose that we can construct that shop of Madame Pace piece by piece here? (*To* THE FATHER.) You said a white room with flowered wallpaper, didn't you?
THE FATHER	Yes.
THE MANAGER	Well then. We've got the furniture right more or less. Bring that little table a bit further forward. (*The* STAGE HANDS *obey the order. To* PROPERTY MAN.) You go and find an envelope, if possible, a pale blue one; and give it to that gentleman. (*Indicates* THE FATHER.)
PROPERTY MAN	An ordinary envelope?
THE MANAGER AND THE FATHER	Yes, yes, an ordinary envelope.
PROPERTY MAN	At once, sir. (*Exit.*)
THE MANAGER	Ready, everyone! First scene—the Young Lady. (*The* LEADING LADY *comes forward.*) No, no, you must wait. I meant her.

	(*Indicating* THE STEP-DAUGHTER.) You just watch—
THE STEP-DAUGHTER	(*Adding at once.*) How I shall play it, how I shall live it!...
LEADING LADY	(*Offended.*) I shall live it also, you may be sure, as soon as I begin!
THE MANAGER	(*With his hands to his head.*) Ladies and gentlemen, if you please! No more useless discussions! Scene I: the young lady with Madame Pace: Oh! (*Looks around as if lost.*) And this Madame Pace, where is she?
THE FATHER	She isn't with us, sir.
THE MANAGER	Then what the devil's to be done?
THE FATHER	But she is alive too.
THE MANAGER	Yes, but where is she?
THE FATHER	One minute. Let me speak! (*Turning to the* ACTRESSES.) If these ladies would be so good as to give me their hats for a moment....
THE ACTRESSES	(*Half surprised, half laughing, in chorus.*) What? Why?

	Our hats? What does he say?
THE MANAGER	What are you going to do with the ladies' hats? (*The* ACTORS *laugh.*)
THE FATHER	Oh nothing. I just want to put them on these pegs for a moment. And one of the ladies will be so kind as to take off her mantle....
THE ACTORS	Oh, what d'you think of that? Only the mantle? He must be mad.
SOME ACTRESSES	But why? Mantles as well?
THE FATHER	To hang them up here for a moment. Please be so kind, will you?
THE ACTRESSES	(*Taking off their hats, one or two also their cloaks, and going to hang them on the racks.*) After all, why not? There you are! This is really funny. We've got to put them on show.
THE FATHER	Exactly; just like that, on show.
THE MANAGER	May we know why?
THE FATHER	I'll tell you. Who knows if, by arranging the stage for her, she does not come here herself, attracted by the very articles of her

trade? (*Inviting the* ACTORS *to look towards the exit at back of stage.*) Look! Look!

(*The door at the back of stage opens and* MADAME PACE *enters and takes a few steps forward. She is a fat, oldish woman with puffy oxygenated hair. She is rouged and powdered, dressed with a comical elegance in black silk. Round her waist is a long silver chain from which hangs a pair of scissors.* THE STEP-DAUGHTER *runs over to her at once amid the stupor of the* ACTORS.)

THE STEP-DAUGHTER	(*Turning towards her.*) There she is! There she is!
THE FATHER	(*Radiant.*) It's she! I said so, didn't I? There she is!
THE MANAGER	(*Conquering his surprise, and then becoming indignant.*) What sort of a trick is this?
LEADING MAN	(*Almost at the same time.*) What's going to happen next?
JUVENILE LEAD	Where does *she* come from?
L'INGÉNUE	They've been holding her in reserve, I guess.
LEADING LADY	A vulgar trick!

THE FATHER (*Dominating the protests.*) Excuse me, all of you! Why are you so anxious to destroy in the name of a vulgar, commonplace sense of truth, this reality which comes to birth attracted and formed by the magic of the stage itself, which has indeed more right to live here than you, since it is much truer than you—if you don't mind my saying so? Which is the actress among you who is to play Madame Pace? Well, here is Madame Pace herself. And you will allow, I fancy, that the actress who acts her will be less true than this woman here, who is herself in person. You see my daughter recognized her and went over to her at once. Now you're going to witness the scene!

(*But the scene between* THE STEP-DAUGHTER *and* MADAME PACE *has already begun despite the protest of the* ACTORS *and the reply of* THE FATHER. *It has begun quietly, naturally, in a manner impossible for the stage. So when the* ACTORS, *called to attention by* THE FATHER, *turn round and see* MADAME PACE, *who has placed one hand under* THE STEP-DAUGHTER'S *chin to raise her head, they observe her at first with great attention, but hearing her speak in an unintelligible manner their interest begins to wane.*)

THE MANAGER Well? well?

LEADING MAN	What does she say?
LEADING LADY	One can't hear a word.
JUVENILE LEAD	Louder! Louder please!
THE STEP-DAUGHTER	(*Leaving* MADAME PACE, *who smiles a Sphinx-like smile, and advancing towards the* ACTORS.) Louder? Louder? What are you talking about? These aren't matters which can be shouted at the top of one's voice. If I have spoken them out loud, it was to shame him and have my revenge. (*Indicates* THE FATHER.) But for Madame it's quite a different matter.
THE MANAGER	Indeed? indeed? But here, you know, people have got to make themselves heard, my dear. Even we who are on the stage can't hear you. What will it be when the public's in the theatre? And anyway, you can very well speak up now among yourselves, since we shan't be present to listen to you as we are now. You've got to pretend to be alone in a room at the back of a shop where no one can hear you.

(THE STEP-DAUGHTER *coquettishly and with a touch of malice makes a sign of disagreement two or three times with her finger.*)

THE MANAGER: What do you mean by no?

THE STEP-DAUGHTER: (*Sotto voce, mysteriously.*) There's someone who will hear us if she (*Indicating* MADAME PACE.) speaks out loud.

THE MANAGER: (*In consternation.*) What? Have you got someone else to spring on us now? (*The* ACTORS *burst out laughing.*)

THE FATHER: No, no sir. She is alluding to me. I've got to be here—there behind that door, in waiting; and Madame Pace knows it. In fact, if you will allow me, I'll go there at once, so I can be quite ready. (*Moves away.*)

THE MANAGER: (*Stopping him.*) No! Wait! wait! We must observe the conventions of the theatre. Before you are ready....

THE STEP-DAUGHTER: (*Interrupting him.*) No, get on with it at once! I'm just dying, I tell you, to act this scene. If he's ready, I'm more than ready.

THE MANAGER: (*Shouting.*) But, my dear young lady, first of all, we must have the scene between you and this lady... (*Indicates* MADAME PACE.) Do you understand?...

THE STEP-DAUGHTER: Good Heavens! She's been telling me what you know already: that mamma's work is

	badly done again, that the material's ruined; and that if I want her to continue to help us in our misery I must be patient....
MADDAME PACE	(*Coming forward with an air of great importance.*) Yes indeed, sir, I no wanta take advantage of her, I no wanta be hard....
	(*Note. Madame Pace is supposed to talk in a jargon half Italian, half Spanish*)
THE MANAGER	(*Alarmed.*) What? What? She talks like that? (*The* ACTORS *burst out laughing again.*)
THE STEP-DAUGHTER	(*Also laughing.*) Yes yes, that's the way she talks, half English, half Italian! Most comical it is!
MADDAME PACE	Itta seem not verra polite gentlemen laugha atta me eef I trya best speaka English.
THE MANAGER	*Diamine!* Of course! Of course! Let her talk like that! Just what we want. Talk just like that, Madam, if you please! The effect will be certain. Exactly what was wanted to put a little comic relief into the crudity of the situation. Of course she talks like that! Magnificent!
THE STEP-DAUGHTER	Magnificent? Certainly! When certain suggestions are made to one in language of that kind, the effect is certain, since it seems almost a joke. One feels inclined to laugh

	when one hears her talk about an "old signore" "who wanta talka nicely with you." Nice old signore, eh, Madame?
MADDAME PACE	Not so old my dear, not so old! And even if you no lika him, he won't make any scandal!
THE MOTHER	(*Jumping up amid the amazement and consternation of the* ACTORS *who had not been noticing her. They move to restrain her.*) You old devil! You murderess!
THE STEP-DAUGHTER	(*Running over to calm her* MOTHER.) Calm yourself, mother, calm yourself! Please don't....
THE FATHER	(*Going to her also at the same time.*) Calm yourself! Don't get excited! Sit down now!
THE MOTHER	Well then, take that woman away out of my sight!
THE STEP-DAUGHTER	(*To* THE MANAGER.) It is impossible for my mother to remain here.
THE FATHER	(*To* THE MANAGER.) They can't be here together. And for this reason, you see: that woman there was not with us when we came.... If they are on together, the whole thing is given away inevitably, as you see.
THE	It doesn't matter. This is only a first rough

MANAGER	sketch—just to get an idea of the various points of the scene, even confusedly.... (*Turning to* THE MOTHER *and leading her to her chair.*) Come along, my dear lady, sit down now, and let's get on with the scene. ... (*Meanwhile,* THE STEP-DAUGHTER, *coming forward again, turns to* MADAME PACE.)
THE STEP-DAUGHTER	Come on, Madame, come on!
MADDAME PACE	(*Offended.*) No, no, *grazie*. I not do anything witha your mother present.
THE STEP-DAUGHTER	Nonsense! Introduce this "old signore" who wants to talk nicely to me. (*Addressing the company imperiously.*) We've got to do this scene one way or another, haven't we? Come on! (*To* MADAME PACE.) You can go!
MADAME PACE	Ah yes! I go'way! I go'way! Certainly! (*Exits furious.*)
THE STEP-DAUGHTER	(*To* THE FATHER.) Now you make your entry. No, you needn't go over here. Come here. Let's suppose you've already come in. Like that, yes! I'm here with bowed head, modest like. Come on! Out with your voice! Say "Good morning, Miss" in that peculiar tone, that special tone....
THE	Excuse me, but are you the Manager, or am

MANAGER I? (*To THE FATHER, who looks undecided and perplexed.*) Get on with it, man! Go down there to the back of the stage. You needn't go off. Then come right forward here.

(*THE FATHER does as he is told, looking troubled and perplexed at first. But as soon as he begins to move, the reality of the action affects him, and he begins to smile and to be more natural. The ACTORS watch intently.*)

THE MANAGER (*Sotto voce, quickly to the PROMPTER in his box.*) Ready! ready? Get ready to write now.

THE FATHER (*Coming forward and speaking in a different tone.*) Good afternoon, Miss!

THE STEP-DAUGHTER (*Head bowed down slightly, with restrained disgust.*) Good afternoon!

THE FATHER (*Looks under her hat which partly covers her face. Perceiving she is very young, he makes an exclamation, partly of surprise, partly of fear lest he compromise himself in a risky adventure.*) "Ah… but… ah… I say … this is not the first time that you have come here, is it?"

THE STEP-DAUGHTER (*Modestly.*) No sir.

THE FATHER You've been here before, eh? (*Then seeing her nod agreement.*) More than once? (*Waits

	for her to answer, looks under her hat, smiles, and then says.) Well then, there's no need to be so shy, is there? May I take off your hat?
THE STEP-DAUGHTER	(*Anticipating him and with veiled disgust.*) No sir... I'll do it myself. (*Takes it off quickly.*)
	(THE MOTHER, *who watches the progress of the scene with* THE SON *and the other two children who cling to her, is on thorns; and follows with varying expressions of sorrow, indignation, anxiety, and horror the words and actions of the other two. From time to time she hides her face in her hands and sobs.*)
THE MOTHER	Oh, my God, my God!
THE FATHER	(*Playing his part with a touch of gallantry.*) Give it to me! I'll put it down. (*Takes hat from her hands.*) But a dear little head like yours ought to have a smarter hat. Come and help me choose one from the stock, won't you?
L'INGÉNUE	(*Interrupting.*) I say... those are our hats you know.
THE MANAGER	(*Furious.*) Silence! silence! Don't try and be funny, if you please.... We're playing the scene now I'd have you notice. (*To* THE STEP-

DAUGHTER.)	Begin again, please!
THE STEP-DAUGHTER	(*Continuing.*) No thank you, sir.
THE FATHER	Oh, come now. Don't talk like that. You must take it. I shall be upset if you don't. There are some lovely little hats here; and then—Madame will be pleased. She expects it, anyway, you know.
THE STEP-DAUGHTER	No, no! I couldn't wear it!
THE FATHER	Oh, you're thinking about what they'd say at home if they saw you come in with a new hat? My dear girl, there's always a way round these little matters, you know.
THE STEP-DAUGHTER	(*All keyed up.*) No, it's not that. I couldn't wear it because I am... as you see... you might have noticed.... (*Showing her black dress.*)
THE FATHER	... in mourning! Of course: I beg your pardon: I'm frightfully sorry....
THE STEP-DAUGHTER	(*Forcing herself to conquer her indignation and nausea.*) Stop! Stop! It's I who must thank you. There's no need for you to feel mortified or specially sorry. Don't think any more of what I've said. (*Tries to smile.*) I must forget that I am dressed so....

THE MANAGER	(*Interrupting and turning to the* PROMPTER.) Stop a minute! Stop! Don't write that down. Cut out that last bit. (*Then to the* THE FATHER *and* THE STEP-DAUGHTER.) Fine! it's going fine! (*To* THE FATHER *only*.) And now you can go on as we arranged. (*To the* ACTORS.) Pretty good that scene, where he offers her the hat, eh?
THE STEP-DAUGHTER	The best's coming now. Why can't we go on?
THE MANAGER	Have a little patience! (*To the* ACTORS.) Of course, it must be treated rather lightly.
LEADING MAN	Still, with a bit of go in it!
LEADING LADY	Of course! It's easy enough! (*To* LEADING MAN.) Shall you and I try it now?
LEADING MAN	Why, yes! I'll prepare my entrance. (*Exit in order to make his entrance.*)
THE MANAGER	(*To* LEADING LADY.) See here! The scene between you and Madame Pace is finished. I'll have it written out properly after. You remain here... oh, where are you going?
LEADING LADY	One minute. I want to put my hat on again. (*Goes over to hat-rack and puts her hat on her head.*)

THE MANAGER	Good! You stay here with your head bowed down a bit.
THE STEP-DAUGHTER	But she isn't dressed in black.
LEADING LADY	But I shall be, and much more effectively than you.
THE MANAGER	(*To* THE STEP-DAUGHTER.) Be quiet please, and watch! You'll be able to learn something. (*Clapping his hands.*) Come on! come on! Entrance, please!
	(*The door at rear of stage opens, and the* LEADING MAN *enters with the lively manner of an old gallant. The rendering of the scene by the* ACTORS *from the very first words is seen to be quite a different thing, though it has not in any way the air of a parody. Naturally,* THE STEP-DAUGHTER *and* THE FATHER, *not being able to recognize themselves in the* LEADING LADY *and the* LEADING MAN, *who deliver their words in different tones and with a different psychology, express, sometimes with smiles, sometimes with gestures, the impression they receive.*)
LEADING MAN	Good afternoon, Miss....
THE FATHER	(*At once unable to contain himself.*) No! no!

(THE STEP-DAUGHTER *noticing the way the* LEADING MAN *enters, bursts out laughing.*)

THE MANAGER (*Furious.*) Silence! And you please just stop that laughing. If we go on like this, we shall never finish.

THE STEP-DAUGHTER Forgive me, sir, but it's natural enough. This lady (*Indicating* LEADING LADY.) stands there still; but if she is supposed to be me, I can assure you that if I heard anyone say "Good afternoon" in that manner and in that tone, I should burst out laughing as I did.

THE FATHER Yes, yes, the manner, the tone....

THE MANAGER Nonsense! Rubbish! Stand aside and let me see the action.

LEADING MAN If I've got to represent an old fellow who's coming into a house of an equivocal character....

THE MANAGER Don't listen to them, for Heaven's sake! Do it again! It goes fine. (*Waiting for the* ACTORS *to begin again.*) Well?

LEADING MAN Good afternoon, Miss.

LEADING LADY Good afternoon.

LEADING MAN	(*Imitating the gesture of* THE FATHER *when he looked under the hat, and then expressing quite clearly first satisfaction and then fear.*) Ah, but... I say... this is not the first time that you have come here, is it?
THE MANAGER	Good, but not quite so heavily. Like this: (*Acts himself.*) "This isn't the first time that you have come here."... (*To* LEADING LADY.) And you say: "No, sir."
LEADING LADY	No, sir.
LEADING MAN	You've been here before, more than once.
THE MANAGER	No, no, stop! Let her nod "yes" first.
	"You've been here before, eh?" (*The* LEADING LADY *lifts up her head slightly and closes her eyes as though in disgust. Then she inclines her head twice.*)
THE STEP-DAUGHTER	(*Unable to contain herself.*) Oh my God! (*Puts a hand to her mouth to prevent herself from laughing.*)
THE MANAGER	(*Turning round.*) What's the matter?
THE STEP-	Nothing, nothing!

DAUGHTER

THE MANAGER: (*To* LEADING MAN.) Go on!

LEADING MAN: You've been here before, eh? Well then, there's no need to be so shy, is there? May I take off your hat?

(*The* LEADING MAN *says this last speech in such a tone and with such gestures that* THE STEP-DAUGHTER, *though she has her hand to her mouth, cannot keep from laughing*)

LEADING LADY: (*Indignant.*) I'm not going to stop here to be made a fool of by that woman there.

LEADING MAN: Neither am I! I'm through with it!

THE MANAGER: (*Shouting to* THE STEP-DAUGHTER.) Silence! for once and all, I tell you!

THE STEP-DAUGHTER: Forgive me! forgive me!

THE MANAGER: You haven't any manners: that's what it is! You go too far.

THE FATHER: (*Endeavouring to intervene.*) Yes, it's true, but excuse her....

THE MANAGER: Excuse what? It's absolutely disgusting.

THE FATHER   Yes, sir, but believe me, it has such a strange effect when....

THE MANAGER   Strange? Why strange? Where is it strange?

THE FATHER   No, sir; I admire your actors—this gentleman here, this lady; but they are certainly not us!

THE MANAGER   I should hope not. Evidently they cannot be you, if they are actors.

THE FATHER   Just so: actors! Both of them act our parts exceedingly well. But, believe me, it produces quite a different effect on us. They want to be us, but they aren't, all the same.

THE MANAGER   What is it then anyway?

THE FATHER   Something that is... that is theirs—and no longer ours....

THE MANAGER   But naturally, inevitably. I've told you so already.

THE FATHER   Yes, I understand... I understand....

THE MANAGER   Well then, let's have no more of it! (*Turning to the* ACTORS.) We'll have the rehearsals by ourselves, afterwards, in the ordinary way. I never could stand rehearsing with the author present. He's never satisfied! (*Turning to* THE FATHER *and* THE STEP-DAUGHTER.) Come on! Let's get on with it again; and try and see if you can't keep from laughing.

THE STEP-DAUGHTER Oh, I shan't laugh any more. There's a nice little bit coming for me now: you'll see.

THE MANAGER Well then: when she says "Don't think any more of what I've said. I must forget, etc.," you (*Addressing* THE FATHER.) come in sharp with "I understand, I understand"; and then you ask her....

THE STEP-DAUGHTER (*Interrupting.*) What?

THE MANAGER Why she is in mourning.

THE STEP-DAUGHTER Not at all! See here: when I told him that it was useless for me to be thinking about my wearing mourning, do you know how he answered me? "Ah well," he said "then let's take off this little frock."

THE MANAGER Great! Just what we want, to make a riot in the theatre!

THE STEP-DAUGHTER But it's the truth!

THE What does that matter? Acting is our

MANAGER	business here. Truth up to a certain point, but no further.
THE STEP-DAUGHTER	What do you want to do then?
THE MANAGER	You'll see, you'll see! Leave it to me.
THE STEP-DAUGHTER	No sir! What you want to do is to piece together a little romantic sentimental scene out of my disgust, out of all the reasons, each more cruel and viler than the other, why I am what I am. He is to ask me why I'm in mourning; and I'm to answer with tears in my eyes, that it is just two months since papa died. No sir, no! He's got to say to me; as he did say: "Well, let's take off this little dress at once." And I; with my two months' mourning in my heart, went there behind that screen, and with these fingers tingling with shame....
THE MANAGER	(*Running his hands through his hair.*) For Heaven's sake! What are you saying?
THE STEP-DAUGHTER	(*Crying out excitedly.*) The truth! The truth!
THE MANAGER	It may be. I don't deny it, and I can understand all your horror; but you must surely see that you can't have this kind of thing on the stage. It won't go.

THE STEP-
DAUGHTER

Not possible, eh? Very well! I'm much obliged to you—but I'm off!

THE MANAGER

Now be reasonable! Don't lose your temper!

THE STEP-
DAUGHTER

I won't stop here! I won't! I can see you've fixed it all up with him in your office. All this talk about what is possible for the stage … I understand! He wants to get at his complicated "cerebral drama," to have his famous remorses and torments acted; but I want to act my part, *my part*!

THE MANAGER

(*Annoyed, shaking his shoulders.*) Ah! Just *your* part! But, if you will pardon me, there are other parts than yours: His (*Indicating* THE FATHER.) and hers! (*Indicating* THE MOTHER.) On the stage you can't have a character becoming too prominent and overshadowing all the others. The thing is to pack them all into a neat little framework and then act what is actable. I am aware of the fact that everyone has his own interior life which he wants very much to put forward. But the difficulty lies in this fact: to set out just so much as is necessary for the stage, taking the other characters into consideration, and at the same time hint at the unrevealed interior life of each. I am willing to admit, my dear young lady, that from your point of view it would be a fine idea if each character could tell the public all his troubles in a nice monologue or a regular one hour lecture. (*Good humoredly.*) You must restrain yourself, my dear, and in your own interest, too; because this fury of yours, this exaggerated disgust you show, may make a bad impression, you know. After you have confessed to me that there were others before him at Madame Pace's and more than once....

THE STEP-DAUGHTER (*Bowing her head, impressed.*) It's true. But remember those others mean him for me all the same.

THE MANAGER (*Not understanding.*) What? The others? What do you mean?

THE STEP-DAUGHTER For one who has gone wrong, sir, he who was responsible for the first fault is responsible for all that follow. He is responsible for my faults, was, even before I was born. Look at him, and see if it isn't true!

THE MANAGER Well, well! And does the weight of so much responsibility seem nothing to you? Give him a chance to act it, to get it over!

THE STEP-DAUGHTER How? How can he act all his "noble remorses" all his "moral torments," if you want to spare him the horror of being discovered one day—after he had asked her what he did ask her—in the arms of her, that already fallen woman, that child, sir, that child he used to watch come out of school? (*She is moved.*)

(THE MOTHER *at this point is overcome with emotion, and breaks out into a fit of crying. All are touched. A long pause.*)

THE STEP-DAUGHTER (*As soon as* THE MOTHER *becomes a little quieter, adds resolutely and gravely.*) At present, we are unknown to the public. Tomorrow, you will act us as you wish, treating us in your own manner. But do you really want to see drama, do you want to see it flash out as it really did?

THE MANAGER Of course! That's just what I do want, so I can use as much of it as is possible.

THE STEP-DAUGHTER Well then, ask that Mother there to leave us.

THE MOTHER (*Changing her low plaint into a sharp cry.*) No! No! Don't permit it, sir, don't permit it!

THE MANAGER But it's only to try it.

THE MOTHER I can't bear it. I can't.

THE MANAGER But since it has happened already... I don't understand!

THE
MOTHER
It's taking place now. It happens all the time. My torment isn't a pretended one. I live and feel every minute of my torture. Those two children there—have you heard them speak? They can't speak any more. They cling to me to keep my torment actual and vivid for me. But for themselves, they do not exist, they aren't any more. And she (*Indicating* THE STEP-DAUGHTER.) has run away, she has left me, and is lost. If I now see her here before me, it is only to renew for me the tortures I have suffered for her too.

THE
FATHER
The eternal moment! She (*Indicating* THE STEP-DAUGHTER.) is here to catch me, fix me, and hold me eternally in the stocks for that one fleeting and shameful moment of my life. She can't give it up! And you sir, cannot either fairly spare me it.

THE
MANAGER
I never said I didn't want to act it. It will form, as a matter of fact, the nucleus of the whole first act right up to her surprise. (*Indicates* THE MOTHER.)

THE
FATHER
Just so! This is my punishment: the passion in all of us that must culminate in her final cry.

THE STEP-
DAUGHTER
I can hear it still in my ears. It's driven me mad, that cry!—You can put me on as you like; it doesn't matter. Fully dressed, if you

like—provided I have at least the arm bare; because, standing like this (*She goes close to* THE FATHER *and leans her head on his breast.*) with my head so, and my arms round his neck, I saw a vein pulsing in my arm here; and then, as if that live vein had awakened disgust in me, I closed my eyes like this, and let my head sink on his breast. (*Turning to* THE MOTHER.) Cry out mother! Cry out! (*Buries head in* THE FATHER's *breast, and with her shoulders raised as if to prevent her hearing the cry, adds in tones of intense emotion.*) Cry out as you did then!

THE MOTHER (*Coming forward to separate them.*) No! My daughter, my daughter! (*And after having pulled her away from him.*) You brute! you brute! She is my daughter! Don't you see she's my daughter?

THE MANAGER (*Walking backwards towards footlights.*) Fine! fine! Damned good! And then, of course—curtain!

THE FATHER (*Going towards him excitedly.*) Yes, of course, because that's the way it really happened.

THE MANAGER (*Convinced and pleased.*) Oh, yes, no doubt about it. Curtain here, curtain!

(*At the reiterated cry of* THE MANAGER, *the* MACHINIST *lets the curtain down, leaving* THE

MANAGER and THE FATHER in front of it before the footlights)

THE MANAGER The darned idiot! I said "curtain" to show the act should end there, and he goes and lets it down in earnest. (*To THE FATHER, while he pulls the curtain back to go on to the stage again.*) Yes, yes, it's all right. Effect certain! That's the right ending. I'll guarantee the first act at any rate.

Act III

(*When the curtain goes up again, it is seen that the stage hands have shifted the bit of scenery used in the last part, and have rigged up instead at the back of the stage a drop, with some trees, and one or two wings. A portion of a fountain basin is visible.* THE MOTHER *is sitting on the Right with the two children by her side.* THE SON *is on the same side, but away from the others. He seems bored, angry, and full of shame.* THE FATHER *and* THE STEP-DAUGHTER *are also seated towards the Right front. On the other side (Left) are the* ACTORS, *much in the positions they occupied before the curtain was lowered. Only* THE MANAGER *is standing up in the middle of the stage, with his hand closed over his mouth in the act of meditating.*)

THE MANAGER (*Shaking his shoulders after a brief pause.*) Ah yes: the second act! Leave it to me, leave it all to me as we arranged, and you'll see! It'll go fine!

THE STEP- Our entry into his house (*Indicates* THE

DAUGHTER	FATHER.) in spite of him.... (*Indicates* THE SON.)
THE MANAGER	(*Out of patience.*) Leave it to me, I tell you!
THE STEP-DAUGHTER	Do let it be clear, at any rate, that it is in spite of my wishes.
THE MOTHER	(*From her corner, shaking her head.*) For all the good that's come of it....
THE STEP-DAUGHTER	(*Turning towards her quickly.*) It doesn't matter. The more harm done us, the more remorse for him.
THE MANAGER	(*Impatiently.*) I understand! Good Heavens! I understand! I'm taking it into account.
THE MOTHER	(*Supplicatingly.*) I beg you, sir, to let it appear quite plain that for conscience sake I did try in every way....
THE STEP-DAUGHTER	(*Interrupting indignantly and continuing for* THE MOTHER.)... to pacify me, to dissuade me from spiting him. (*To Manager.*) Do as she wants: satisfy her, because it is true! I enjoy it immensely. Anyhow, as you can see, the meeker she is, the more she tries to get at his heart, the more distant and aloof does he become.
THE MANAGER	Are we going to begin this second act or not?

THE STEP-DAUGHTER	I'm not going to talk any more now. But I must tell you this: you can't have the whole action take place in the garden, as you suggest. It isn't possible!
THE MANAGER	Why not?
THE STEP-DAUGHTER	Because he (*Indicates* THE SON *again.*) is always shut up alone in his room. And then there's all the part of that poor dazed-looking boy there which takes place indoors.
THE MANAGER	Maybe! On the other hand, you will understand—we can't change scenes three or four times in one act.
LEADING MAN	They used to once.
THE MANAGER	Yes, when the public was up to the level of that child there.
LEADING LADY	It makes the illusion easier.
THE FATHER	(*Irritated.*) The illusion! For Heaven's sake, don't say illusion. Please don't use that word, which is particularly painful for us.
THE MANAGER	(*Astounded.*) And why, if you please?

THE FATHER   It's painful, cruel, really cruel; and you ought to understand that.

THE MANAGER   But why? What ought we to say then? The illusion, I tell you, sir, which we've got to create for the audience....

LEADING MAN   With our acting.

THE MANAGER   The illusion of a reality.

THE FATHER   I understand; but you, perhaps, do not understand us. Forgive me! You see... here for you and your actors, the thing is only—and rightly so... a kind of game....

LEADING LADY   (*Interrupting indignantly.*) A game! We're not children here, if you please! We are serious actors.

THE FATHER   I don't deny it. What I mean is the game, or play, of your art, which has to give, as the gentleman says, a perfect illusion of reality.

THE MANAGER   Precisely—!

THE FATHER   Now, if you consider the fact that we, (*Indicates himself and the other five* CHARACTERS.) as we are, have no other reality outside of this illusion....

THE MANAGER (*Astonished, looking at his* ACTORS, *who are also amazed.*) And what does that mean?

THE FATHER (*After watching them for a moment with a wan smile.*) As I say, sir, that which is a game of art for you is our sole reality. (*Brief pause. He goes a step or two nearer* THE MANAGER *and adds.*) But not only for us, you know, by the way. Just you think it over well. (*Looks him in the eyes.*) Can you tell me who you are?

THE MANAGER (*Perplexed, half smiling.*) What? Who am I? I am myself.

THE FATHER And if I were to tell you that that isn't true, because you are I...?

THE MANAGER I should say you were mad—! (*The* ACTORS *laugh.*)

THE FATHER You're quite right to laugh: because we are all making believe here. (*To* THE MANAGER.) And you can therefore object that it's only for a joke that that gentleman there, (*Indicates the* LEADING MAN.) who naturally is himself, has to be me, who am on the contrary myself—this thing you see here. You see I've caught you in a trap! (*The* ACTORS *laugh.*)

THE MANAGER (*Annoyed.*) But we've had all this over once before. Do you want to begin again?

THE FATHER	No, no! That wasn't my meaning! In fact, I should like to request you to abandon this game of art (*Looking at the* LEADING LADY *as if anticipating her.*) which you are accustomed to play here with your actors, and to ask you seriously once again: who are you?
THE MANAGER	(*Astonished and irritated, turning to his* ACTORS.) If this fellow here hasn't got a nerve! A man who calls himself a character comes and asks me who I am!
THE FATHER	(*With dignity, but not offended.*) A character, sir, may always asks a man who he is. Because a character has really a life of his own, marked with his especial characteristics; for which reason he is always "somebody." But a man—I'm not speaking of you now—may very well be "nobody."
THE MANAGER	Yes, but you are asking these questions of me, the boss, the manager! Do you understand?
THE FATHER	But only in order to know if you, as you really are now, see yourself as you once were with all the illusions that were yours then, with all the things both inside and outside of you as they seemed to you—as they were then indeed for you. Well, sir, if you think of all those illusions that mean

nothing to you now, of all those things which don't even *seem* to you to exist any more, while once they *were* for you, don't you feel that—I won't say these boards—but the very earth under your feet is sinking away from you when you reflect that in the same way this *you* as you feel it today—all this present reality of yours—is fated to seem a mere illusion to you tomorrow?

THE MANAGER (*Without having understood much, but astonished by the specious argument.*) Well, well! And where does all this take us anyway?

THE FATHER Oh, nowhere! It's only to show you that if we (*Indicating the* CHARACTERS.) have no other reality beyond the illusion, you too must not count overmuch on your reality as you feel it today, since, like that of yesterday, it may prove an illusion for you tomorrow.

THE MANAGER (*Determining to make fun of him.*) Ah, excellent! Then you'll be saying next that you, with this comedy of yours that you brought here to act, are truer and more real than I am.

THE FATHER (*With the greatest seriousness.*) But of course; without doubt!

THE MANAGER Ah, really?

THE
FATHER

Why, I thought you'd understand that from the beginning.

THE
MANAGER

More real than I?

THE
FATHER

If your reality can change from one day to another....

THE
MANAGER

But everyone knows it can change. It is always changing, the same as anyone else's.

THE
FATHER

(*With a cry.*) No, sir, not ours! Look here! That is the very difference! Our reality doesn't change: it can't change! It can't be other than what it is, because it is already fixed for ever. It's terrible. Ours is an immutable reality which should make you shudder when you approach us if you are really conscious of the fact that your reality is a mere transitory and fleeting illusion, taking this form today and that tomorrow, according to the conditions, according to your will, your sentiments, which in turn are controlled by an intellect that shows them to you today in one manner and tomorrow... who knows how?... Illusions of reality represented in this fatuous comedy of life that never ends, nor can ever end! Because if tomorrow it were to end... then why, all would be finished.

THE
MANAGER
Oh for God's sake, will you *at least* finish with this philosophizing and let us try and shape this comedy which you yourself have brought me here? You argue and philosophize a bit too much, my dear sir. You know you seem to me almost, almost... (*Stops and looks him over from head to foot.*) Ah, by the way, I think you introduced yourself to me as a—what shall... we say—a "character," created by an author who did not afterward care to make a drama of his own creations.

THE
FATHER
It is the simple truth, sir.

THE
MANAGER
Nonsense! Cut that out, please! None of us believes it, because it isn't a thing, as you must recognize yourself, which one can believe seriously. If you want to know, it seems to me you are trying to imitate the manner of a certain author whom I heartily detest—I warn you—although I have unfortunately bound myself to put on one of his works. As a matter of fact, I was just starting to rehearse it, when you arrived. (*Turning to the* ACTORS.) And this is what we've gained—out of the frying-pan into the fire!

THE
FATHER
I don't know to what author you may be alluding, but believe me I feel what I think; and I seem to be philosophizing only for

those who do not think what they feel, because they blind themselves with their own sentiment. I know that for many people this self-blinding seems much more "human"; but the contrary is really true. For man never reasons so much and becomes so introspective as when he suffers; since he is anxious to get at the cause of his sufferings, to learn who has produced them, and whether it is just or unjust that he should have to bear them. On the other hand, when he is happy, he takes his happiness as it comes and doesn't analyse it, just as if happiness were his right. The animals suffer without reasoning about their sufferings. But take the case of a man who suffers and begins to reason about it. Oh no! it can't be allowed! Let him suffer like an animal, and then—ah yes, he is "human!"

THE MANAGER Look here! Look here! You're off again, philosophizing worse than ever.

THE FATHER Because I suffer, sir! I'm not philosophizing: I'm crying aloud the reason of my sufferings.

THE MANAGER (*Makes brusque movement as he is taken with a new idea.*) I should like to know if anyone has ever heard of a character who gets right out of his part and perorates and speechifies as you do. Have you ever heard of a case? I haven't.

THE
FATHER
You have never met such a case, sir, because authors, as a rule, hide the labour of their creations. When the characters are really alive before their author, the latter does nothing but follow them in their action, in their words, in the situations which they suggest to him; and he has to will them the way they will themselves—for there's trouble if he doesn't. When a character is born, he acquires at once such an independence, even of his own author, that he can be imagined by everybody even in many other situations where the author never dreamed of placing him; and so he acquires for himself a meaning which the author never thought of giving him.

THE
MANAGER
Yes, yes, I know this.

THE
FATHER
What is there then to marvel at in us? Imagine such a misfortune for characters as I have described to you: to be born of an author's fantasy, and be denied life by him; and then answer me if these characters left alive, and yet without life, weren't right in doing what they did do and are doing now, after they have attempted everything in their power to persuade him to give them their stage life. We've all tried him in turn, I, she (*Indicating* THE STEP-DAUGHTER.) and she. (*Indicating* THE MOTHER.)

THE STEP-DAUGHTER	It's true. I too have sought to tempt him, many, many times, when he has been sitting at his writing table, feeling a bit melancholy, at the twilight hour. He would sit in his armchair too lazy to switch on the light, and all the shadows that crept into his room were full of our presence coming to tempt him. (*As if she saw herself still there by the writing table, and was annoyed by the presence of the ACTORS.*) Oh, if you would only go away, go away and leave us alone—mother here with that son of hers—I with that Child—that Boy there always alone—and then I with him (*Just hints at THE FATHER.*)—and then I alone, alone… in those shadows! (*Makes a sudden movement as if in the vision she has of herself illuminating those shadows she wanted to seize hold of herself.*) Ah! my life! my life! Oh, what scenes we proposed to him—and I tempted him more than any of the others!
THE FATHER	Maybe. But perhaps it was your fault that he refused to give us life: because you were too insistent, too troublesome.
THE STEP-DAUGHTER	Nonsense! Didn't he make me so himself? (*Goes close to THE MANAGER to tell him as if in confidence.*) In my opinion he abandoned us in a fit of depression, of disgust for the ordinary theatre as the public knows it and likes it.

THE SON Exactly what it was, sir; exactly that!

THE FATHER Not at all! Don't believe it for a minute. Listen to me! You'll be doing quite right to modify, as you suggest, the excesses both of this girl here, who wants to do too much, and of this young man, who won't do anything at all.

THE SON No, nothing!

THE MANAGER You too get over the mark occasionally, my dear sir, if I may say so.

THE FATHER I? When? Where?

THE MANAGER Always! Continuously! Then there's this insistence of yours in trying to make us believe you are a character. And then too, you must really argue and philosophize less, you know, much less.

THE FATHER Well, if you want to take away from me the possibility of representing the torment of my spirit which never gives me peace, you will be suppressing me: that's all. Every true man, sir, who is a little above the level of the beasts and plants does not live for the sake of living, without knowing how to live; but he lives so as to give a meaning and a value of his own to life. For me this is *everything*. I cannot give up this, just to represent a mere fact as she (*Indicating* THE STEP-DAUGHTER.)

wants. It's all very well for her, since her "vendetta" lies in the "fact." I'm not going to do it. It destroys my raison d'être.

THE MANAGER. Your raison d'être! Oh, we're going ahead fine! First she starts off, and then you jump in. At this rate, we'll never finish.

THE FATHER. Now, don't be offended! Have it your own way—provided, however, that within the limits of the parts you assign us each one's sacrifice isn't too great.

THE MANAGER. You've got to understand that you can't go on arguing at your own pleasure. Drama is action, sir, action and not confounded philosophy.

THE FATHER. All right. I'll do just as much arguing and philosophizing as everybody does when he is considering his own torments.

THE MANAGER. If the drama permits! But for Heaven's sake, man, let's get along and come to the scene.

THE STEP-DAUGHTER. It seems to me we've got too much action with our coming into his house. (*Indicating* THE FATHER.) You said, before, you couldn't change the scene every five minutes.

THE MANAGER. Of course not. What we've got to do is to combine and group up all the facts in one simultaneous, close-knit, action. We can't have it as you want, with your little brother wandering like a ghost from room to room, hiding behind doors and meditating a project which—what did you say it did to him?

THE STEP-DAUGHTER Consumes him, sir, wastes him away!

THE MANAGER Well, it may be, And then at the same time, you want the little girl there to be playing in the garden... one in the house, and the other in the garden: isn't that it?

THE STEP-DAUGHTER Yes, in the sun, in the sun! That is my only pleasure: to see her happy and careless in the garden after the misery and squalor of the horrible room where we all four slept together. And I had to sleep with her—I, do you understand?—with my vile contaminated body next to hers; with her folding me fast in her loving little arms. In the garden, whenever she spied me, she would run to take me by the hand. She didn't care for the big flowers, only the little ones; and she loved to show me them and pet me.

THE MANAGER Well then, we'll have it in the garden. Everything shall happen in the garden; and we'll group the other scenes there. (*Calls a* STAGE HAND.) Here, a backcloth with trees and something to do as a fountain basin.

(*Turning round to look at the back of the stage.*) Ah, you've fixed it up. Good! (*To* THE STEP-DAUGHTER.) This is just to give an idea, of course. The Boy, instead of hiding behind the doors, will wander about here in the garden, hiding behind the trees. But it's going to be rather difficult to find a child to do that scene with you where she shows you the flowers. (*Turning to the* YOUTH.) Come forward a little, will you please? Let's try it now! Come along! come along! (*Then seeing him come shyly forward, full of fear and looking lost.*) It's a nice business, this lad here. What's the matter with him? We'll have to give him a word or two to say. (*Goes close to him, puts a hand on his shoulders, and leads him behind one of the trees.*) Come on! come on! Let me see you a little! Hide here... yes, like that. Try and show your head just a little as if you were looking for someone.... (*Goes back to observe the effect, when* THE BOY *at once goes through the action.*) Excellent! fine! (*Turning to* THE STEP-DAUGHTER.) Suppose the little girl there were to surprise him as he looks round, and run over to him, so we could give him a word or two to say?

THE STEP-DAUGHTER   It's useless to hope he will speak, as long as that fellow there is here.... (*Indicates* THE SON.) You must send him away first.

THE SON   (*Jumping up.*) Delighted! delighted! I don't

ask for anything better. (*Begins to move away.*)

THE MANAGER (*At once stopping him.*) No! No! Where are you going? Wait a bit!

(THE MOTHER *gets up alarmed and terrified at the thought that he is really about to go away. Instinctively she lifts her arms to prevent him, without, however, leaving her seat.*)

THE SON (*To* THE MANAGER *who stops him.*) I've got nothing to do with this affair. Let me go please! Let me go!

THE MANAGER What do you mean by saying you've got nothing to do with this?

THE STEP-DAUGHTER (*Calmly, with irony.*) Don't bother to stop him: he won't go away.

THE FATHER He has to act the terrible scene in the garden with his mother.

THE SON (*Suddenly resolute and with dignity.*) I shall act nothing at all. I've said so from the very beginning. (*To* THE MANAGER.) Let me go!

THE STEP-DAUGHTER (*Going over to* THE MANAGER.) Allow me? (*Puts down* THE MANAGER*'s arm which is restraining* THE SON.) Well, go away then, if you want to! (THE SON *looks at her with* contempt and hatred. *She laughs and says.*) You see, he can't, he can't go away! He is obliged to stay here, indissolubly bound to the chain. If I, who fly off when that happens which has to happen, because I can't bear him—if I am still here and support that face and expression of his, you can well imagine that he is unable to move. He has to remain here, has to stop with that nice father of his, and that mother whose only son he is. (*Turning to* THE MOTHER.) Come on, mother, come along! (*Turning to* THE MANAGER *to indicate her.*) You see, she was getting up to keep him back. (*To* THE MOTHER, *beckoning her with her hand.*) Come on! come on! (*Then to* THE MANAGER.) You can imagine how little she wants to show these actors of yours what she really feels; but so eager is she to get near him that.... There, you see? She is willing to act her part. (*And in fact,* THE MOTHER *approaches him; and as soon as* THE STEP-DAUGHTER *has finished speaking, opens her arms to signify that she consents.*)

THE SON (*Suddenly.*) No! no! If I can't go away, then I'll stop here; but I repeat: I act nothing!

THE FATHER (*To* THE MANAGER *excitedly.*) You can force him, sir.

THE SON Nobody can force me.

THE FATHER	I can.
THE STEP-DAUGHTER	Wait a minute, wait.... First of all, the baby has to go to the fountain.... (*Runs to take* THE CHILD *and leads her to the fountain.*)
THE MANAGER	Yes, yes of course; that's it. Both at the same time.

(*The* SECOND LADY LEAD *and the* JUVENILE LEAD *at this point separate themselves from the group of* ACTORS. *One watches* THE MOTHER *attentively; the other moves about studying the movements and manner of* THE SON *whom he will have to act.*)

THE SON	(*To* THE MANAGER.) What do you mean by both at the same time? It isn't right. There was no scene between me and her. (*Indicates* THE MOTHER.) Ask her how it was!
THE MOTHER	Yes, it's true. I had come into his room....
THE SON	Into my room, do you understand? Nothing to do with the garden.
THE MANAGER	It doesn't matter. Haven't I told you we've got to group the action?
THE SON	(*Observing the* JUVENILE LEAD *studying him.*) What do you want?

JUVENILE LEAD	Nothing! I was just looking at you.
THE SON	(*Turning towards the* SECOND LADY LEAD.) Ah! she's at it too: to re-act her part! (*Indicating* THE MOTHER.)
THE MANAGER	Exactly! And it seems to me that you ought to be grateful to them for their interest.
THE SON	Yes, but haven't you yet perceived that it isn't possible to live in front of a mirror which not only freezes us with the image of ourselves, but throws our likeness back at us with a horrible grimace?
THE FATHER	That is true, absolutely true. You must see that.
THE MANAGER	(*To* SECOND LADY LEAD *and the* JUVENILE LEAD.) He's right! Move away from them!
THE SON	Do as you like. I'm out of this!
THE MANAGER	Be quiet, you, will you? And let me hear your mother! (*To* THE MOTHER.) You were saying you had entered....
THE MOTHER	Yes, into his room, because I couldn't stand it any longer. I went to empty my heart to him of all the anguish that tortures me.... But as soon as he saw me come in....
THE SON	Nothing happened! There was no scene. I

	went away, that's all! I don't care for scenes!
THE MOTHER	It's true, true. That's how it was.
THE MANAGER	Well now, we've got to do this bit between you and him. It's indispensable.
THE MOTHER	I'm ready... when you are ready. If you could only find a chance for me to tell him what I feel here in my heart.
THE FATHER	(*Going to* THE SON *in a great rage.*) You'll do this for your mother, for your mother, do you understand?
THE SON	(*Quite determined.*) I do nothing!
THE FATHER	(*Taking hold of him and shaking him.*) For God's sake, do as I tell you! Don't you hear your mother asking you for a favour? Haven't you even got the guts to be a son?
THE SON	(*Taking hold of* THE FATHER.) No! No! And for God's sake stop it, or else.... (*General agitation.* THE MOTHER, *frightened, tries to separate them.*)
THE MOTHER	(*Pleading.*) Please! please!
THE FATHER	(*Not leaving hold of* THE SON.) You've got to obey, do you hear?

THE SON (*Almost crying from rage.*) What does it mean, this madness you've got? (*They separate.*) Have you no decency, that you insist on showing everyone our shame? I won't do it! I won't! And I stand for the will of our author in this. He didn't want to put us on the stage, after all!

THE MANAGER Man alive! You came here....

THE SON (*Indicating* THE FATHER.)*He* did! I didn't!

THE MANAGER Aren't you here now?

THE SON It was his wish, and he dragged us along with him. He's told you not only the things that did happen, but also things that have never happened at all.

THE MANAGER Well, tell me then what did happen. You went out of your room without saying a word?

THE SON Without a word, so as to avoid a scene!

THE MANAGER And then what did you do?

THE SON Nothing ... walking in the garden.... (*Hesitates for a moment with expression of gloom.*)

THE MANAGER	(*Coming closer to him, interested by his extraordinary reserve.*) Well, well... walking in the garden....
THE SON	(*Exasperated.*) Why on earth do you insist? It's horrible! (THE MOTHER *trembles, sobs, and looks towards the fountain.*)
THE MANAGER	(*Slowly observing the glance and turning towards* THE SON *with increasing apprehension.*) The baby?
THE SON	There in the fountain....
THE FATHER	(*Pointing with tender pity to* THE MOTHER.) She was following him at the moment....
THE MANAGER	(*To* THE SON *anxiously.*) And then you....
THE SON	I ran over to her; I was jumping in to drag her out when I saw something that froze my blood... the boy there standing stock still, with eyes like a madman's, watching his little drowned sister, in the fountain! (THE STEP-DAUGHTER *bends over the fountain to hide* THE CHILD. *She sobs.*) Then.... (*A revolver shot rings out behind the trees where* THE BOY *is hidden.*)
THE MOTHER	(*With a cry of terror runs over in that direction together with several of the* ACTORS *amid general confusion.*) My son! My son!

(*Then amid the cries and exclamations one hears her voice.*) Help! Help!

THE MANAGER (*Pushing the ACTORS aside while they lift up THE BOY and carry him off.*) Is he really wounded?

SOME ACTORS He's dead! dead!

OTHER ACTORS No, no, it's only make believe, it's only pretence!

THE FATHER (*With a terrible cry.*) Pretence? Reality, sir, reality!

THE MANAGER Pretence? Reality? To hell with it all! Never in my life has such a thing happened to me. I've lost a whole day over these people, a whole day!

(*Curtain.*)

www.ingramcontent.com/pod-product-compliance
Lightning Source LLC
LaVergne TN
LVHW040107080526
838202LV00045B/3802